CONTENTS

Illustrated by Tony Gibson
Additional illustrations by Martin Newton

Designed by Teresa Foster
Additional designs by Tony Gibson

Consultant: Sue Becklake

SCHOLASTIC INC.
New York Toronto London Auckland

D0249385

a
ment
year.
nce light
year, or
on, million
scie... ...illion, million
answer ... ...ht travels at a
and the jot ... of 186,000 miles
astronomer is ...,000 km) per
understand the ...ond.
Universe.

...ion km).

It takes eleven hours to
reach the furthest planet
in our Solar System,
which is Pluto.

One of the family

The Earth on which we
live is one of a family of
nine planets moving
around the Sun. Together
they are known as the
Solar System. The Sun
itself is one very
ordinary star in our
galaxy, the Milky Way,
which contains about
100,000 million stars
altogether.

Sun

Mercury

Venus

Earth

Mars

Jupiter

Saturn

Uranus

Neptune

Pluto

One among many

Our own galaxy measures
about 950,000 million,
million km (590,000 million,
million miles) across. It is
only one among millions of
other galaxies. All the
galaxies and the space
around them make up the
Universe.

As far as we can see

THE END OF
THE
UNIVERSE?

The greatest distance
astronomers can see into
the Universe is about
15,000 million light
years, although this is
not necessarily the edge
of the Universe. It might
not even have a
boundary.

Amazing But True

If it was possible to
travel in a spacecraft at
the speed of light, you
could go around the
Earth seven times in
just one second.

The light reaching us now from our nearest star set off over four years ago. At present rocket speeds it would probably take thousands of years to get to the nearest star and back.

The scale of the Universe

The distances in the Universe are so great that it is difficult to imagine them. If the Sun was the size of a ball 6 ft (1.8 m) across, then Pluto, the most distant planet in our Solar System, would be the size of a pea 4.7 miles (7.6 km) away. But our nearest star would be about 32,313 miles (52,000 km) away.

We've only just begun

The exploration of space by satellites and spacecraft is helping scientists learn more about our neighboring worlds in the Solar System and about the Universe as a whole. But so far we have only been able to explore two other planets in our Solar System with unmanned spacecraft.

Future meetings

In the future we may be able to travel as far as the stars and land on their planets. Some stars may have planets on which other beings live whom we may be able to visit or contact by radio.

Now read on

This book tells you about some of the discoveries that have been made and the possible plans for the future, some of which may happen in your own lifetime.

Going up Our Universe at different heights

A 1 km (0.6 miles): low altitude

B 10,000 km (6,210 miles): high.

C 1 million km (621,000 miles): Earth-Moon system.

D 10 million, million km (6 million, million miles): 1 light year.

E 100,000 light years: Milky Way galaxy.

F 15,000 million light years: limits of the observable Universe.

The Solar System

The Sun's family

All the planets surrounding the Sun are members of the Sun's family, known as the Solar System. The Sun lies at the center of the family and orbiting (circling) around it are the planets and their moons and also the asteroids.

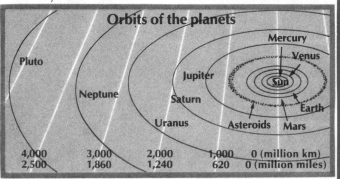

Orbits of the planets

Pluto
Neptune
Uranus
Jupiter
Saturn
Mercury
Venus
Sun
Earth
Asteroids
Mars

| 4,000 | 3,000 | 2,000 | 1,000 | 0 (million km) |
| 2,500 | 1,860 | 1,240 | 620 | 0 (million miles) |

The Sun's diameter of 865,000 miles (1,392,000 km) is about 109 times that of Earth's and 10 times that of Jupiter's. If the Sun were represented by a beach ball with a 20 in (50cm) diameter, Mars would be the size of a small pea about 180 ft (55 m) away and Jupiter would be the size of a golfball 919 ft (280 m) away.

Birth in a cloud

Many scientists think that the Solar System was formed from a cloud of gas and dust about 4,600 million years ago. The Sun formed in the center while the planets grew from balls of gas around it.

Gas condenses

Sun born

Planets form

Solar System born

Merry-go-round

All the members of the Solar System move about other objects. The moons are circling their parent planets, the planets circle the Sun while each spins about its axis at the same time. The Sun also spins and the whole Solar System is moving around the galaxy it lies in.

Messenger of the gods

Named after the speedy messenger of the Roman gods, Mercury travels around the Sun at the fastest speed of all the planets, about 107,030 mph (172,248 kph).

The Sun gives off huge amounts of deadly radiation, but we are protected from the worst blasts by a magnetic cage called the magnetosphere that surrounds the Earth. Inside this cage, two doughnut-shaped belts trap the electric particles. These are called the Van Allen belts after James Van Allen, their discoverer.

Data		
Planet	Rotational period (around axis)	Orbital period (around Sun)
Mercury	58.7 days	88 days
Venus	243 days	224.7 days
Earth	23.93 hrs	365.25 days
Mars	24.62 hrs	687 days
Jupiter	9.92 hrs	11.9 years
Saturn	10.23 hrs	29.5 years
Uranus	17 hrs	84 years
Neptune	18 hrs	165 years
Pluto	6.4 days	248 years

Brightest and faintest

Viewed from Earth, by far the brightest of the planets visible to the naked eye is Venus. It is often called the "evening star." The faintest planet is Pluto. It can only be seen through a telescope.

The unique planet

The Earth is a very special planet because it is the only place in the Solar System, and the only known place in the entire Universe, to support life. If it was closer to the Sun it would be too hot to support life and if it was farther away it would be too cold.

Fast spinner

Jupiter is the fastest spinning planet in our Solar System. If you could stand on the equator of the planet, you would be travelling at a speed of 28,273 mph (45,500 kph), compared with the Earth's speed of 325 mph (523 kph).

The Sun
One among millions

The Sun is a star, one of 100,000 million stars in our galaxy, the Milky Way. Although it is a very ordinary star in the galaxy, it is very important in our Solar System; without it there would be no life on Earth.

Sizing up the Sun

If the Sun was the size of a large orange, the Earth would be the size of a tiny seed about 33 ft (10 m) away.

Great ball of fire

The Sun is mainly made up of the lightest gas, called hydrogen. It burns up 770 million tons of hydrogen every second in nuclear reactions at its center. Scientists believe the Sun loses 4.4 million tons of gas every second, which is about the weight of one million elephants.

A Corona (outer part of the Sun's atmosphere) — 36 million °F.

B Chromosphere (6,000 miles deep/9,600 km) — 7,200°F to more than 90,000°F at the top.

C Photosphere (249 miles deep/400 km) — 10,000°F.

D Convective zone (where gases move around).

E Radiative zone.

F Solar interior — 59 million°F. Nuclear reactions take place here.

Amazing But True

One second of the energy given off by the Sun is 13 million times greater than the average amount of electricity used each year in the USA. All the Earth's oil, coal and wood supplies would fuel the Sun for only a few days.

A long car drive

The distance of the Sun from Earth is just under 93 million miles (150 million km). This distance is called an astronomical unit. If you drove a car at 55 mph (88 kph) from the Earth to the Sun, it would take 193 years.

Dangerous heat

The temperature at the center of the Sun reaches 27 million °F (15 million °C). If a pinhead was this hot, it would ignite and destroy everything for 60 miles (100 km) around it.

DID YOU KNOW?

Just one square centimeter of the Sun's surface shines with the brightness of 232,500 candles.

Deadly breeze

The Sun gives off a stream of particles charged with electricity. This is called the solar wind and is estimated to blow more than twice as far as Pluto, the farthest planet in the Solar System.

Light shows

Glowing colored lights, called aurorae, can sometimes be seen in the skies of the north and south poles. They happen when the electric particles from the Sun bump into the gases in the Earth's atmosphere and make them glow.

The Sun's beauty spots

Areas of gas that are cooler than the rest of the surface appear as dark patches on the Sun and are called sunspots. They only seem dark in comparison to the brilliant surrounding surface. Eight Earths can fit into the area of one sunspot.

Fiery fountains

Fountains of burning hydrogen and helium gas, called solar prominences, flare up in the Sun's chromosphere. The greatest solar prominence ever recorded reached a height of 250,000 miles (402,000 km), more than the distance from Earth to the Moon.

Why a battle ended

Eclipses of the Sun take place when the Sun, Moon and Earth are all lined up so that the Moon blocks out the sunlight. In 585BC an eclipse happened in the middle of a battle between the Lydians and Medes. The armies made peace.

The Moon

Data

Diameter at the equator:
2,086 mi

Mass: 0.0123 (Earth = 1.
It would take 81 Moons
to equal the mass of the
Earth.)
Surface gravity: 0.17
(Earth = 1)

Distance from Earth
furthest: 244,020 mi
nearest: 213,840 mi
average: 230,400 mi
Rotational period around
Earth: 27.3 Earth-days

Phases of the Moon

From Earth, the Moon
seems to change shape,
from a sliver to a full
Moon and back to a
sliver again. This is
because we see different
amounts of the Moon's
sunlit side as it moves
around the Earth. The
different shapes are
called phases and the
Moon goes through its
phases in 29.5 days.

Pockmarked surface

About 500,000 Moon
craters can be seen
through the most
powerful telescopes. It
would take someone
about 400 hours to count
all of them – and just
those on the face that we
can see.

A Scottish crater

The largest crater we can
see on the Moon is
called Bailly and covers
an area of about 26,000
square miles (67,300
square km). If Bailly
was brought down to
Earth, Scotland could sit
comfortably inside it.

Our nearest neighbor

The Moon is the closest
neighbor to Earth. Its
average distance from
Earth is only 239,000
miles (384,000 km). A
train travelling at 100
mph (161 kph) would
take 99.5 days to cover
the distance.

DID YOU KNOW?

The Moon takes just
over 27 days to travel
around the Earth. It
always keeps the same
half facing the Earth. The
far side of the Moon had
never been seen until
the USSR spacecraft
Luna 3 took the first
photographs of it in 1959.

Seas without water

The dark areas you can see on the Moon's surface are called "seas." There is no water there but millions of years ago they were covered by volcanic lava. Some are very big. The Ocean of Storms is larger than the Mediterranean.

As dry as dust

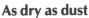

The Moon has no atmosphere and contains no water. Its soil is so dry that nothing will grow in it. But scientists have found that with air and water, plants can grow in Moon soil on Earth.

Dead quiet

The Moon is a completely silent place. Noises cannot be heard as there is no air to carry sound from one place to another.

Precious stones

The various Apollo astronauts who landed on the Moon brought back to Earth a total of 842 lb (382 kg) of Moon rocks and dust. Divided into the total cost of the Apollo space program, the samples of Moon rock and dust cost around $1,896,000 per ounce.

Staying the same

Unlike the Earth, which has been continuously worn away, the surface of the Moon has not been attacked by wind and water. The rocks brought back to Earth by astronauts had probably been lying in the same position on the surface of the Moon for 3,000 million years without moving a fraction.

Amazing But True

Footprints left on the Moon by the Apollo astronauts will probably be visible for at least 10 million years.

Moonquivers

There are earthquakes on the Moon known as moonquakes, but they are very weak compared to our earthquakes. About 3,000 occur each year, but all the moonquakes in one year would produce enough energy for just a small fireworks display.

Gravity and tides

The pull of gravity of the Earth on the Moon keeps the Moon circling around the Earth. But the Moon's gravity also pulls the water in the Earth's seas towards it, causing the Earth's tides. If the Moon was closer to Earth the pull of its gravity would be much stronger and the tides would flood the coastlines of the world.

Mercury, Venus and Mars

Data

Planet	Diameter at the equator	Mass	Orbital speed (around Sun)	Surface temperatures	Satellites
Mercury	2,927 mi	0.055 (Earth = 1)	28.7 mi/sec	662°F	0
Venus	7,260 mi	0.815	21.0 mi/sec	896°F	0
Mars	4,068 mi	0.107	14.5 mi/sec	−9°F	2

The inner planets

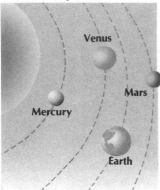

Mercury, Venus and Mars, along with the Earth, form a group of four rocky planets unlike the others. They are known as the inner planets because they are the nearest to the Sun.

Hotter than a desert

Mercury is the closest planet to the Sun. Because of this, it has scorching daytime temperatures of up to 662°F (350°C). This is over seven times hotter than the hottest temperature ever recorded on Earth — 136°F (57.7°C) at Azizia, Libya in 1922.

Freezer cold

The temperature on Mercury at night can plunge to −274°F (−170°C) because there is no blanket of atmosphere to trap the heat. This is more than seven times colder than the temperature inside the freezer compartment of a refrigerator.

DID YOU KNOW?

Mercury has a core of iron, slightly bigger than our Moon. At recent world production figures for iron, it would take about 6,500 million years to mine all the iron in Mercury's core.

Not really an atmosphere

Although Mercury is surrounded by a thin layer of helium gas, there is so little of it that the amount collected from a 4 mile (6.4 km) diameter sphere would be just enough to fill a child's small balloon.

Clouds of acid

Although Venus and Earth are about the same size, their atmospheres are completely different. Venus' atmosphere is made up mostly of carbon dioxide gas, which is poisonous, and contains sulphuric acid in its clouds.

Deep atmosphere diving

Venus' atmosphere is so thick that at the planet's surface the pressure is 90 times that on Earth. On Earth, the atmospheric pressure measures 14.7 lb/in² (1.03 kg/cm²). On Venus, the same area has a pressure of 1,323 lbs (600 kg). This is the pressure a diver would experience at 264 ft (80 m) beneath the sea.

Back-to-front

Venus rotates east to west, in the opposite direction to all the other planets. This means that the Sun rises in the west and sets in the east.

Amazing But True

There is so little water in the Martian atmosphere that if all of it was collected together it would fit into the Serpentine Lake, London, UK.

Greenhouse effect

The atmosphere on Venus traps the heat in a similar way to a greenhouse so that the temperature reaches about 932°F (500°C).

Mountain high

One of the highest mountains in the Solar System is found on Venus. It is called the Maxwell Montes and is more than 1.2 miles (2 km) higher than Mt. Everest.

Canyon long

Mars has the largest canyon in the Solar System, called the Mariner Valley. It is 13 times longer than the Grand Canyon, and would stretch from one side of the USA to the other.

Midget moons

Mars has two tiny moons, called Phobos and Deimos. Deimos is so small and its gravity so weak that people could launch themselves into space by reaching a speed of 22 mph (36 kph).

Jupiter and Saturn

Data	Jupiter	Saturn
Diameter at the equator	85,800 mi	72,000 mi
Mass	318 (Earth = 1)	95
Orbital speed (around Sun)	7.9 mi/sec	5.8 mi/sec
Cloud top temperatures	−238°F	−292°C
Number of satellites	16	21

Sizing up Jupiter

Jupiter is much smaller than the Sun. If the Sun's diameter was equal to a giant tractor tire 69 in (175 cm) in diameter, then Jupiter would be the size of a ball 7 in (18 cm) in diameter and the Earth would be the size of a small marble about 0.4 in (1 cm) in diameter.

Similar planets

Jupiter and Saturn are members of a group of four planets, known as the "gas giants," which are very different from the inner planets. They have small rocky centers, surrounded by liquid hydrogen and covered with thick, cloudy atmospheres.

The giant planet

Jupiter is the largest planet in our Solar System. Jupiter is more than 1,300 times bigger than Earth and bigger than all the other planets put together.

The Great Red Spot

The reddish patch on Jupiter is known as the Great Red Spot and was first recorded in the 17th century. It is the biggest hurricane in the Solar System with swirling clouds about 24,000 miles (38,500 km) long by 7,000 miles (11,000 km) wide. It is as big as three Earths.

Fat stomach

Jupiter spins around very quickly on its axis, taking less than 10 hours to make one turn. This forces the equator to bulge out so that the planet looks like a squashed ball.

Heart pressure

The core of Jupiter is about the size of Earth and has a temperature of about 54,000°F (30,000°C). The pressure at the core is more than 30 million times higher than the Earth's atmosphere. If anyone flew to Jupiter and then landed on the surface, they would be crushed by the pressure straight away.

Jupiter is so big that if a bicyclist set out to travel non-stop once around it at a speed of 6 mph (9.6 kph), the journey would take more than five years (1,935 days) to complete.

Inside-out moon

The most explosive object in the Solar System is one of Jupiter's moons, called Io. Geologists estimate that the volcanoes on its surface throw up enough material every 3,000 years to cover the entire surface with a thin layer about 0.4 in (1 cm) thick. So Io is continually turning itself inside out.

Speedy moon

The fastest-moving moon in the Solar System, known as J3, travels at a speed of about 70,400 miles (113,600 km) per hour. A person travelling at this speed could fly from Bombay in India to Port Said in Egypt in 2 minutes 11 seconds.

DID YOU KNOW?

Saturn is the second biggest planet in the Solar System and it is 95 times heavier than Earth. The volume of Saturn is 744 times that of Earth.

Hurricane winds

The winds that blow around Saturn's equator are ten times stronger than the average hurricane on Earth, travelling at 1,100 mph (1,770 kph).

Record rings

Saturn is one of the most beautiful planets in the Solar System. It is surrounded by rings made up of millions of icy particles. The ice particles are like tiny mirrors and are very thin compared to their 171,000 mile (275,000 km) diameter. They are only about 300 ft (100 m) thick. On this scale, a phonograph record 0.06 in (1.5 mm) thick would be 2.5 miles (4 km) across.

Lighter than water

Saturn is composed mostly of hydrogen and helium gas and liquid, like Jupiter. But it is smaller than Jupiter. It has the lowest density of all the planets in the Solar System. If it was the size of a tennis ball it would be able to float in a bucket of water.

Uranus, Neptune and Pluto

Data	Uranus	Neptune	Pluto
Diameter at the equator	31,200 mi	29,400 mi	Approx. 1,440 mi
Mass	14.54 (Earth = 1)	17.2	0.002?
Orbital speed around Sun	4.1 mi/sec	3.2 mi/sec	2.8 mi/sec
Surface temperatures	− 346°F	− 364°F	− 382°F
Satellites	15	2	1

Little and large

Uranus and Neptune are a second pair of "gas giants," though smaller than Jupiter and Saturn. Pluto is a small, solid planet, probably more like the rocky inner planets (Mercury, Venus, Earth and Mars). They are all far too cold for anything to live on their surfaces.

Green with methane

The atmospheres surrounding Uranus and Neptune contain hydrogen and helium, like those of Jupiter and Saturn. But their atmospheres also contain methane gas, which makes them look green from Earth.

Amazing But True

One of the strangest things about Uranus is that it rolls around the Sun on its side, while all the other planets spin around like tops. This means that either Uranus' northern or southern hemisphere

will face the Sun and will receive almost constant sunlight, while the other remains in darkness. This creates the Solar System's longest seasons, summers and winters – about 21 years long.

New discovery

People used to think that the most distant planet in the Solar System was Saturn. But in 1781 an astronomer called Sir William Herschel discovered a faint planet which was later named Uranus. It was the first planet to be discovered since the Ancient Greeks.

Blacker than black

In 1977, astronomers discovered that Uranus has a set of narrow rings. There are now thought to be 10 of these. They are made of about the darkest material known in the Solar System.

Not quite a twin

Neptune was first seen in 1846. It is almost the twin of Uranus, but it is slightly smaller and it does not have Uranus' tilt.

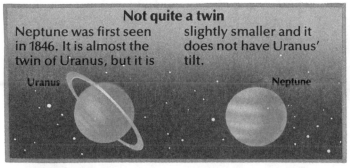

Uranus

Neptune

Old first birthday

A baby born on Pluto (if that was possible) would have to wait 248 Earth years before it reached its first birthday.

Long plane journey

The average distance of Neptune from the Sun is 2,800 million miles (4,500 million km). This is 30 times the distance between Earth and the Sun. If an airplane flew at 1,100 mph (1,770 kph), it would take 289 years to travel from Neptune to the Sun.

DID YOU KNOW?

A person on Neptune would never live for one Neptune year. The Neptune year is the time it takes Neptune to travel once around the Sun – 164.8 Earth years.

The smallest planet

Pluto was discovered in 1930. With a diameter of 1,500 miles (2,400 km) it is smaller than our Moon, making it the smallest and lightest planet in the Solar System

Stretched orbit

Pluto has a very strange path around the Sun. While the routes of the other planets are almost circles, Pluto's is more elongated. Because of its strange orbit, Pluto is closer to the Sun between 1979 and 1999 than Neptune, making Neptune the most distant planet from Earth during those years.

Uranus

Sun

Neptune

Pluto

Close companion

Pluto has a very close companion, a moon called Charon that was discovered in 1978 and that lies only 12,500 miles (20,000 km) from Pluto. Its diameter is about 500 miles (800 km), making it the largest moon compared to its planet in the Solar System.

Spaced out

For most of the time, Pluto is the furthest planet from Earth. An airplane travelling at a speed of 1,125 mph (1,810 kph) would take about 370 years to travel from Earth to Pluto.

Asteroids, comets and meteors

Stone belt

Between the inner planets (Mercury, Venus, Earth and Mars) and the outer planets (Jupiter, Saturn, Uranus, Neptune and Pluto) lies a belt of about 40,000 much smaller irregular planets known as asteroids.

The main comets	
Name	Orbital period around Sun (years)
Schwassmann – Wachmann	16.1
Halley	76.03
D'Arrest	6.2
Encke	3.3
Pons – Winnecke	6.3
Finlay	6.9
Faye	7.4
Tuttle	13.61
Crommelin	27.9

Big lump

The largest asteroid is called Ceres. It measures about 620 miles (1,000 km) in diameter and if it arrived on Earth it could fit onto the surface of France.

Dirty snowballs

Comets are balls of icy particles and dust that come from the most distant parts of the Solar System and travel around the Sun. A comet glows slightly and reflects the light of the Sun. Scientists think that about 100,000 million comets may circle the Sun.

Roaring tail

When a comet approaches the Sun, a huge tail appears behind it. This is made up of gas and dust released from the comet by the heat of the Sun. The comet's tail points away from the Sun because the solar wind blows it away.

Wrapping up Earth

The Great Comet of 1843 had a tail about 200 million miles (330 million km) long. If this tail was wrapped around Earth it would circle the equator about 8,000 times.

Lighter than air

The density of a comet is far less than that of water or air. If all the comets were put together they would weigh no more than the Earth.

Life boat

According to astronomers Chandra Wickramsinghe and Sir Frederick Hoyle, life may have originated far out in space and been brought to Earth aboard a comet which crashed onto the surface.

Signs in the sky

The appearance of Halley's Comet in the sky through the centuries has been regarded as an important sign. It was seen in England in 1066 before the Battle of Hastings and William the Conqueror's battle cry was "A new star, a new king."

Amazing But True

The only living creature known to have been killed by a meteorite was a dog, struck dead at Nakhla, Egypt in 1911.

Streaking rocks

Meteors are small pieces of rock that enter the top of Earth's atmosphere. They do not manage to travel far down and reach the Earth's surface, but burn up about 50 miles (80 km) up in the sky, producing streaks of light known as "shooting stars."

Jumbo meteorite

Meteorites are large chunks of rock that reach the Earth's surface without burning up. Scientists think that they come from asteroids. The largest known meteorite in the world fell to Earth at Hoba West in Namibia, Africa. It measures 9x8 ft (2.7x2.4 m) and weighs about 66 tons, as much as 9 elephants.

Explosive impact

One of the most famous meteorite craters on Earth is the Arizona Crater. It was formed about 22,000 years ago and the force of the explosion when the meteorite hit Earth equalled 1,000 Hiroshima atomic bombs.

Iron from space

Eskimos in Greenland used iron tools for centuries, even though they could not smelt iron. They mined iron in almost pure form from three large meteorites that had fallen on Greenland hundreds of years ago.

DID YOU KNOW?

Meteors burn up in the atmosphere and filter down to Earth as dust. The total weight of the Earth increases in weight from this dust by about 27 tons each day, which adds up to 10,040 tons each year.

The life of stars

Millions of suns

The stars you can see in the night sky are really distant suns. Our Sun is only one very ordinary star among millions of others. The next nearest star to our Solar System is called Proxima Centauri and is 4.25 light years away.

A star is born

Stars are born from the huge clouds of gas and dust known as nebulae that float in the Universe. They begin to grow when part of a cloud forms into a small lump. This grows smaller and hotter until a nuclear reaction starts and the star is born.

Long journey

A car travelling from our Solar System at 55 mph (88.5 kph) would take 52 million years to drive to Proxima Centauri. This is equal to about 722,000 average lifetimes.

Hot heart

The heart of a star is extremely hot and reaches a temperature of about 29 million °F (16 million °C). A grain of sand that hot would kill a person up to 100 miles (161 km) away.

Long-distance call

One of the largest stars known is called Betelgeuse. It has a diameter of 621 million miles (1,000 million km), or about 730 times greater than the Sun. If you made a telephone call from one side to the other, your voice, travelling at the speed of light, would take 55 minutes to reach the other end of the line.

What is a star?

A star shines with its own light. It is made up mostly of hydrogen gas and held together by its own gravity. Reactions in the heart of stars, like those in nuclear bombs, generate heat and light.

Star death

When the hydrogen gas at the center of a star is burned up, it begins to die. It then swells up to a red giant star. When our Sun begins to die it will swell up until it is beyond the Earth's orbit, destroying the entire planet and destroying Mercury and Venus as well.

Little heavyweight

A red giant star then collapses into a ball about the size of the Earth. This is known as a white dwarf star and its gravity is so strong that a large cupful of its material weighs about 550 tons, which is about the weight of two Boeing 747 jumbo jets put together.

Neutron stars

If a star is much bigger than the Sun, the collapse goes beyond the white dwarf stage and does not stop until the star is about 6.25 miles (10 km) across. This is called a neutron star and a pinhead of its material would weigh about 1 million tons. This is about the same weight as two of the world's largest supertankers put together.

Amazing But True

A 9 lb (4 kg) baby would weigh 90,000 million lb (40,000 million kg) on the surface of a neutron star because the gravity is so strong.

Pulsating stars

Some neutron stars spin around very fast, as much as 642 times a second, sending out a beam of radio waves. This type of neutron star is called a pulsar. The first pulsar was discovered in 1968 by a British astronomer called Antony Hewish. He thought it was a message coming from another planet, until more were discovered.

Shrinking to nothing

A dying star at least three times bigger than the Sun goes on shrinking beyond the neutron star stage. Its gravity is so strong that it drags everything back to the star. The star has become a black hole. Black holes are impossible to see because even light cannot escape from them.

Groups of stars

Star families

Some of the stars in our galaxy, like our Sun, are alone with no star companions. But because stars are normally born in groups which gradually drift apart, many are found in pairs or sometimes larger numbers.

Pairs of stars

Double, or binary, stars consist of two stars which circle around each other. Close pairs of stars may take only a day or even less to complete their circuits, but pairs that are far apart may take over a hundred years.

Star clusters

As well as binary stars and small groups, there are larger groups called star clusters. There are two types of cluster, known as open and globular. Open clusters are found in the spiral arms of our galaxy and usually contain several hundred young stars. Globular clusters are found near the center of our galaxy and are much more compact groups containing up to a million older stars.

The Seven Sisters

About 1,000 open clusters are in our galaxy. The Pleiades is one such cluster, containing about 400 stars. It is also known as the Seven Sisters and can easily be found in the night sky without a telescope.

Amazing But True

There are about 130 globular clusters in our galaxy. Globular clusters are so tightly packed at their centers that if our Earth was placed in the middle of one, the nearest stars would only be light days away, rather than light years. Our night sky would always be as bright as if there was a full moon shining.

The heaviest giants

Plaskett's star, lying about 2,700 light years away from us, is really made up of two giant stars that orbit each other every 14 days. Astronomers think that the largest of the two stars is so big that it is about 55 times heavier than the Sun. A star this weight would be the size of about 18 million Earths or 1,460 million Moons.

A gang of stars

As well as double stars, there are star systems with three or even more members, though not many of these are known. A well-known example, called Castor, contains six stars. Only three stars can be seen with a telescope, two bright and one dim, but each is really a close double star.

DID YOU KNOW?

A nova (meaning "new star") is a star that suddenly flares up to be many times brighter than it was. A really brilliant nova may have been a star which could hardly be seen even with a large telescope. It then suddenly becomes visible to the naked eye but gradually fades again.

Eclipsing stars

Some pairs of stars move around each other so that, seen from Earth, they block out each other's light. These are known as eclipsing binaries and the amount of light we can see goes down during each eclipse.

Mystery giant

One of the mysterious eclipsing binary stars is called Epsilon Aurigae. The two stars revolve around each other every 27 years. One of the stars has never been directly seen but some astronomers believe it may be the largest star known, with a diameter 2,800 times that of the Sun. If it was placed in the middle of our Solar System, the edge of this star would reach as far as Uranus.

Throbbing stars

Eclipsing stars are not the only ones whose brightness goes up and down. There are some stars called the Cepheid variables that actually swell and shrink regularly. As they throb in and out their brightness also rises and falls.

The brightest star

Eta Carinae is an unusual variable star. Astronomers think that it may be a slow nova star. In 1843 it flashed its record brilliance which has been estimated to have been up to six million times brighter than the Sun, making Eta Carinae the most brilliant star ever recorded.

Nebulae

Dusty space

Although the stars in the night sky look close together, they are really separated by huge stretches of space. This space contains very small gas and dust particles known as interstellar matter.

Interstellar matter is much thinner than the air we breathe on Earth. A cup of air contains about 1,000 million, million, million atoms, but a cupful of space gas is so thin that it would contain only about 300 atoms.

Gas and dust clouds

Some of the interstellar matter in space has collected together to form clouds called nebulae (from the Latin for clouds). There are three types of nebula.

Dark nebulae do not shine but, by blocking out the light from the stars behind, they appear as darker patches in the sky.

Reflection nebulae also do not shine but reflect the light from nearby stars.

Many glowing nebulae contain young, hot stars which make the gases glow.

Star nurseries

The oldest stars in our galaxy are concentrated in the central bulge. The younger stars, like our Sun, lie further from the center in the spiral arms. This is the area where stars are born and objects like the Orion, Lagoon and Trifid nebulae are star birthplaces. The dark spots inside may be baby stars.

Galactic babies

Every 18 days, about 20 times a year, our galaxy gives birth to a new star. Every half second a human birth occurs on Earth.

Giant explosions

Some nebulae are formed from the remains of giant star explosions called supernovae. The outer layers of the star are thrown off as clouds of gas which glow. The Crab Nebula is the most famous example of this type and is believed to have been formed in 1054, when Edward the Confessor was King of England.

The Orion Nebula is so huge that if the distance between the Earth and the Sun was represented by 1 in (2.5 cm), the Orion Nebula would be 12.6 miles (20.3 km) in diameter.

Blowing bubbles

A huge cloud of gas called the Cygnus Superbubble lies about 6,500 light years away from our Solar System. Astronomers believe that this superbubble was formed from a number of supernovae explosions over the last three or four million years.

Death and life

Supernovae explosions are so powerful that they are brighter than 1,000 million suns. This type of nebula represents the end of a star's life and new stars will be born from the clouds of gas to continue the cycle of life and death.

A veil of gas

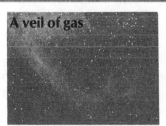

The Veil Nebula lies about 2,500 light years away from us and is probably formed from the remains of a supernova explosion. Astronomers have calculated that the explosion took place about 50,000 years ago, when primitive humans lived on Earth.

Amazing But True

The Orion Nebula in our galaxy is a glowing nebula. It lies about 1,600 light years away from us but it is so bright that it can be seen with the naked eye. It is many times thinner than the air we breathe. If a sample 1 in (2.5 cm) in diameter could be taken all the way through the nebula, the material collected would weigh less than a small coin.

Smoke signals

Ring nebulae are formed from the puffs of gases given off by dying stars when they reach the red giant stage near the end of their lifetimes. The expanding, glowing gases form rings around the stars.

The Milky Way

Our galaxy

Stars are not scattered randomly throughout the Universe, but are grouped together in giant clouds known as galaxies. The Milky Way is the name of the galaxy our Solar System lies in, in one of the spiral arms.

Star town

The Milky Way contains at least 100,000 million stars. Huge distances lie between each one. If each star was the size of the period at the end of this sentence, there would be one star every 3.26 in² (21 cm²), covering an area of about 15.5 square miles. (40 km). This is the size of a small town.

Giant catherine wheel

Because we live inside the Milky Way, it is difficult to see its shape. Astronomers have worked out that the Milky Way is in the shape of a giant spiral measuring about 100,000 light years in diameter. Two starry arms wind around the centers several times like a catherine wheel.

DID YOU KNOW?

The word galaxy comes from the Greek word for milk, "gala." The Ancient Greeks thought the Milky Way was formed from spilt milk from the breast of the goddess Hera when she suckled the baby Herakles (Hercules).

Pot belly

The center of the Milky Way measures about 20,000 light years from one side to the other and bulges up and down. About 40,000 million of the galaxy's stars are concentrated in the center.

Star crashes

Stars at the center of the Milky Way probably collide once every 1,000 years. If the car collision rate on Earth was the same we would have to wait two million years before the first crash, and there would not have been a single one so far in car history.

Cutting it down to size

If our Solar System could fit into a tea cup, the Milky Way would be the size of North America.

Galactic fog

We cannot see deep into the heart of the Milky Way because of huge clouds of gas and dust that block the view. To see the center from Earth would be like trying to see the Moon through a thick cloud of smoke.

Greedy guts

Some astronomers think that a very powerful black hole lies at the center of the Milky Way, equal in weight to four million Suns. Such a black hole would be so powerful that it would capture and destroy the equivalent of 3.3 Earths every year.

Galaxy drive

Our Solar System lies in one of the arms of the Milky Way, about 33,000 light years from the center of the galaxy. If you drove a car from Earth at 100 miles (161 km) per hour it would take a total of about 221,000 million years to reach the center of the Milky Way.

Amazing But True

Our galaxy is so huge that a flash of light travelling at its natural speed of 670 million miles (1,100 million km) per hour would take 100,000 years to go from one side of the galaxy to the other.

Changing shape

The stars of the Milky Way move continuously around the center, but they do not turn like a solid wheel. Stars near the center travel one circuit in only 10 million years, yet out near our Solar System a single

circuit takes about 225 million years. Every time our Solar System moves once around the galaxy, the central stars turn 100 times. This means that the shape of the Milky Way is slowly changing the whole time.

Happy cosmic birthday

A cosmic year is the time it takes our galaxy to cover one complete circuit, about 225 million years. One cosmic year ago, the Earth was at the beginning of the Triassic period, when giant reptiles were replacing sea creatures as the main form of life.

Galaxies

A drop in the ocean of space

Most astronomers believe that galaxies were formed about 14,000 million years ago, about 1,000 million years after the Big Bang (the explosion that formed the Universe). The galaxy we live in is called the Milky Way. There are probably thousands of millions of other galaxies.

The Earth is the third closest planet to the Sun and one of the smaller planets of the Solar System.

The Solar System is tiny when seen in its galaxy, the Milky Way.

The Milky Way itself is insignificant when pictured with the other galaxies.

Types of galaxies

Galaxies come in various shapes. Four main types have been named according to their shapes: spirals, ellipticals, barred spirals and irregular galaxies.

The largest galaxies have diameters of about 500,000 light years but the smallest have diameters of a few thousand light years.

Spiral

Elliptical

Barred spiral

Irregular

DID YOU KNOW?

Galaxies are found in groups or clusters. Many clusters of galaxies are known, some of which contain hundreds of members loosely held together by the force of gravity. The Virgo cluster of galaxies, more than 60 million light years away from us, contains at least 1,000 galaxies. Our cluster consists of only about 20 galaxies.

Continue counting

An average galaxy contains about 100,000 million stars. To count all the stars would take a thousand years at the rate of three a second.

Outshining the Sun

The galaxy known as M87 is the brightest in the Virgo cluster. A mysterious jet of gases streams out of its center about 5,000 light years into space. The brightest point in this jet shines with the strength of 40 million Suns.

Second-rate galaxy

Our galaxy, the Milky Way, is a member of a cluster known as the local group which contains about 20 other galaxies. A galaxy called the Andromeda Spiral is the largest member of the group, with the Milky Way coming a poor second.

Older than humans

The Andromeda Spiral is estimated to be 2.2 million light years from the Milky Way. It is the most distant object visible to the naked eye yet it is still one of the nearest galaxies to us. When you look at Andromeda you are seeing light that started its journey in your direction when mammoths first lived on the Earth's surface.

Amazing But True

Some galaxies are powerful sources of radio waves as well as light. These are known as radio galaxies. Astronomers now think that the radio waves could be caused by huge explosions inside the galaxies.

Calling all quasars

In 1963 radio waves were discovered to be coming from objects that looked like faint stars. These are now called quasars and about 1,300 have so far been discovered. They seem to be small compared to galaxies but up to a thousand times brighter than normal galaxies.

To the edge of time

The most distant object ever seen in the Universe through a telescope is a quasar known as PKS2000-330 and it is thought to be 13,000 million light years away from us. It is racing

away from our galaxy at a speed of about 170,000 miles/sec (273,000 km/sec), about two-thirds the distance from the Earth to the Moon each second.

Origins of the Universe

The Big Bang theory

Most astronomers now believe that the Universe began with a huge explosion, often referred to as the "Big Bang." A tiny point of incredible energy blew apart, scattering hot gases in every direction. Out of this material the galaxies, stars and planets were formed.

Disappearing stars

When their light is examined with special equipment, most stars show something known as red shift. This indicates that the stars are moving away from us and shows that the Universe is still expanding with the force of the Big Bang. When the Universe was 9.5 million years old, it was expanding at nearly the speed of light — 186,000 miles (300,000 km) per second.

The age of the Universe

Once astronomers had measured the speed at which the galaxies are moving outwardly, they could work back to decide how long ago the Universe began. They now generally agree that it started about 15,000 million years ago. If each year was equal to one second, the seconds would add up to almost 475 years.

Time chart

Millions of years		Event
0		Big Bang
1,000		Galaxies begin to form.
4,000		Stars develop within galaxies.
10,000		Our Solar System forms.
11,000		Life begins to form on Earth.
14,650		Human beings (*Homo sapiens*) first appear on Earth.
15,000		Today

A hot pinhead

Astronomers think that the temperature one second after the Big Bang was so hot that it measured about 18,000 million °F. Just a pinhead amount of this very high temperature, with a radius of 0.03937 in (1 mm), would equal over 18 times the entire energy output of the Sun since it was born about 5,000 million years ago.

Starting all over again

Some astronomers believe that the outward-speeding galaxies could slow down and then fall back towards the center. Finally they would collide and create a new explosion. The cycle would be repeated about every 80,000 million years, which means that the next Big Bang could take place in about 65,000 million years' time. This is known as the Oscillating Universe theory.

Some of the particles that make up living things have been found in outer space. One of them is alcohol. Astronomers estimate that a huge cloud in the constellation of Sagittarius contains enough ethyl alcohol to make 10,000 million, million, million, million bottles of whisky.

The mysterious neutrino

Among the most mysterious ingredients of the Universe are neutrinos. They are unimaginably tiny particles, freed one second after the Big Bang. These particles travel at the speed of light and can pass right through Earth without even slowing down. Millions will pass through this page, and through you, in the time it takes you to read it.

Amazing But True

Radio astronomers used to think that the crackling noises picked up on their equipment were caused by pigeon droppings on their radio antennae. But they have now found that space is filled with faint radio waves. These are the dying radio echoes of the Big Bang.

Staying the same

Some astronomers believe that although the Universe is expanding it always looks the same. This is because new galaxies are formed at the center to replace those that are moving outward. This is known as the Steady State theory.

Early astronomy

Farming astronomers

People in ancient times used the position of the Sun and the Moon in the skies to tell them the season of the year, so that they could plan the planting and harvesting of their crops. They built stone monuments thousands of years ago that served as giant calendars, some of which can still be seen in parts of the world today.

Stone calendar

Stonehenge in England was started nearly 4,000 years ago and has different pairs of stones which can be lined up with sunrise and moonrise on different days throughout the year. This monument may have been used to find midsummer and midwinter before the invention of the calendar.

A giant clock

The Great Pyramid of Cheops was built by the Ancient Egyptians in about 2,550BC. It is probably the world's oldest astronomical observatory and as well as being a tomb it was designed to tell the time in hours, days, seasons and even centuries.

Nearly right

The distance around the Earth was first accurately measured by a Greek astronomer called Eratosthenes, who lived from about 276 to 194BC. His figure of about 24,856 miles (40,000 km) almost matched the modern measurement of 24,860 miles (40,007 km).

Using a telescope

In the early 17th century, the Italian scientist Galileo Galilei was the first person to use a telescope in astronomy. Among his discoveries, he first saw four of Jupiter's moons and argued that the planets circled the Sun in the same way as these moons circled Jupiter.

DID YOU KNOW?

The first person to claim that the earth revolves around the Sun was a Greek astronomer called Aristarchos of Samos who lived from about 310 to 250BC. But as everyone believed the Sun moved around the Earth, this idea was not accepted.

The Ptolemaic theory

In about AD150, A Greek astronomer known as Ptolemy stated that the Earth lay stationary at the center of the Universe and the Sun, the Moon and the five known planets (Mercury, Venus, Mars, Jupiter and Saturn) all moved around it. Most people believed this for the next 1,400 years.

The Copernican theory

In 1543, a Polish clergyman called Nicolas Copernicus stated that the Sun was at the center of the Universe and not the Earth. The Earth turned on its axis once a day and travelled around the Sun once a year. But Copernicus still believed that the planets moved around in circles, which is wrong.

Going around in ellipses

Finally, in 1609, Johannes Kepler of Germany figured out the correct movement of the planets. He calculated that the planets moved around the Sun in ellipses (flattened circles) not circles.

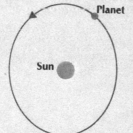

The pull of gravity

The story that the English astronomer Sir Isaac Newton developed his Law of Universal Gravity in 1687 after watching an apple fall to the ground is probably true. He realized that the force which pulled down the apple was the same as the force which keeps the Moon in its path around the Earth and all the planets in their paths around the Sun.

Amazing But True

In the 6th century BC, a Greek philosopher called Heraclitus estimated that the Sun measured only about one-third of 1 ft (meter) across. In fact, it is nearly 870,000 miles (1.4 million km) across.

The world is round

In the 6th century BC, the Greek mathematician Pythagoras claimed that the Earth was a sphere rotating on its axis. But most people thought that the Earth was flat and so few agreed with him.

Modern astronomy

Above the clouds

Many astronomers today work in large observatories built high in mountain ranges. Here they are above most of the clouds and away from the dazzle of street lights so that they can see the night sky more clearly.

Amazing But True

A telescope in the Lick Observatory, USA also serves as a tomb. The refracting telescope is mounted on a pillar that contains the remains of James Lick, who paid for the observatory and who died in 1876.

Increasing the light

Astronomers can see many thousands of stars that are invisible to the naked eye by using telescopes. These are used to magnify distant objects, such as nebulae, and also to collect more light coming from them and reaching the eye.

Lenses and mirrors

Telescopes collect light from stars using either a lens (a refracting telescope) or a mirror (a reflecting telescope). The larger the lens or mirror in a telescope, the more light it can collect and so the more powerful it is. The largest modern telescopes are usually reflectors.

The big one

The world's largest reflecting telescope was built in the 1970s near Zelenchukskaya in the Caucasus Mountains, Russia. Its largest mirror weighs 77 tons and measures 236 in (6 m) across. It is powerful enough to spot the light from a single candle 15,000 miles (24,000 km) away.

Odd one out

One of the strangest telescopes is buried 1 mile (1,500 m) down a mine in South Dakota. At the bottom is a tank containing 88,000 gallons (400,000 liters) of tetrachloroethylene (cleaning fluid). This is used to stop neutrinos, tiny particles given off by the Sun, so that they can be counted by astronomers.

Giant cameras

Photographs of stars and planets were first taken through a telescope in 1840. Photography is now so important in astronomy that many observatories have telescopes which have been designed not to be looked through and can only take photographs.

Colour information

In the 19th century, astronomers first began to study the light from the Sun and stars by splitting it up into its different colors. This is known as spectroscopy. From the colors astronomers can tell the temperature and types of gases in the stars and thus what the stars are made of.

Radio telescopes

Radio telescopes are designed to pick up radio waves coming from distant radio sources. The first true radio telescope was built in 1937. The main type of radio telescope today looks like a giant dish. The radio waves are focused onto the telescope's receiver, above or below the dish.

DID YOU KNOW?

Some radio telescopes, known as interferometers, consist of two or more medium-sized radio telescopes. This is like using a single radio dish several kilometers wide and so gives a much clearer picture of the skies.

The sensitive giant

The world's largest radio telescope is at Arecibo in Puerto Rico. Its dish measures 1,000 ft (305 m) across, wider than three football fields. It can pick up signals as weak as one-hundredth of a millionth of a millionth of a watt. (An ordinary light bulb is 100 watts.)

A faint glimmer

Radio waves from space are very weak. It has been calculated that if the energy reaching us from a quasar – a mysterious type of galaxy that sends out radio waves – were collected by a radio telescope for 10,000 years, there would only be enough to light a small bulb for a fraction of a second.

Astronomy in orbit

Blanket atmosphere

A lot of information from stars never reaches astronomers on the ground because of the blanket of atmosphere that surrounds the Earth. Now that telescopes can be placed above the atmosphere, astronomers can detect invisible waves of energy from stars known as ultra-violet and X-rays which never reach the Earth's surface.

Light bulb power

Most satellites are powered by solar cells, which convert sunlight into electricity. On average, a scientific satellite needs only about 250 watts of power. This is about the amount of power used in two ordinary house light bulbs.

Eyes in the sky

Before satellites carrying telescopes were launched into space, there were three ways of looking at the stars from above the Earth's surface — from airplanes, balloons and rockets. These are all still used, as well as satellites.

Homes in the sky

A space station is a kind of giant satellite where people can live for many days on end without returning to Earth. The Soviet Salyut and the latest Mir series and the American Skylab were launched to carry out scientific experiments and to discover the effect on people of long periods in space.

What they can see

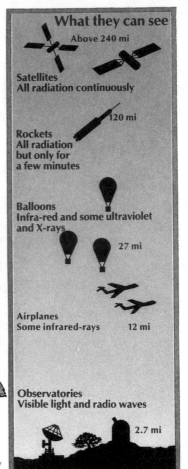

Satellites
All radiation continuously — Above 240 mi

Rockets
All radiation but only for a few minutes — 120 mi

Balloons
Infra-red and some ultraviolet and X-rays — 27 mi

Airplanes
Some infrared-rays — 12 mi

Observatories
Visible light and radio waves — 2.7 mi

A long time in space

The longest time anyone has spent non-stop in space is nearly 237 days. This was achieved in 1984 by three Soviet cosmonauts called Kizim, Solovyov and Atkov in Salyut 7.

The first space station

The first space station, called Salyut 1, was launched by the USSR in 1971. Salyut 6 spent five years in space, the longest time a space station has spent in orbit. It re-entered the Earth's atmosphere and broke up in 1982.

In space, far from the pull of gravity of planets, objects have no weight. This is known as weightlessness. People get a little taller in space because the discs in their backbones are no longer squashed down by the pressure of gravity and their backs stretch a little.

As big as a house

The total size of Skylab, with the Apollo Command and Service modules attached, was about 11,700 cu ft (331.5 cu m), about the same as a small, two-bedroom house.

Spinning and swimming

Small animals were also kept on board Skylab. Two spiders adapted to weightlessness and spun normal webs. Minnows born on Earth swam in a tank in small circles, but those born in space swam normally.

The space ferry

The Space Shuttle is designed mainly as a ferry to carry people and equipment such as satellites into space. The cost of the entire shuttle program so far, $9,900 million, amounts to about $2 for every human being in the world.

Amazing But True

The space telescope is so accurate that if it was placed on Earth it could see a small coin 435 miles (700 km) away. This is about the distance between London, England and Basle, Switzerland. The space telescope should also be able to see if there are any planets circling nearby stars in our galaxy.

The space telescope

The USA is planning to launch a telescope into space using the Space Shuttle. The space telescope will orbit about 373 miles (600 km)

above the Earth and is designed to detect objects 50 times fainter or seven times farther away than anything which can be seen from Earth.

Missions to the Moon

Orbiting football

Sputnik 1 was launched by the Soviets in October 1957 and was the first spacecraft to go into orbit around the Earth. This marks the real beginning of the Space Age and the race to reach the Moon. Sputnik 1 weighed only 185 lb (84 kg), about the weight of an adult, and was the size of a large ball.

Unmanned probes		
Spacecraft	**Date**	**Results**
Luna 2 (USSR)	12 Sep 59	First man-made object to hit the Moon.
Luna 3 (USSR)	4 Oct 59	Flew behind the Moon and took the first photographs of the far side.
Rangers (USA)	1964-65	Photographed the Moon before crashing into the surface.
Luna 9 (USSR)	31 Jan 66	Made the first soft-landing on the Moon and sent back photographs.
Surveyors (USA)	1966-68	Collected information about the surface of the Moon in preparation for manned landings.
Orbiters (USA)	1966-67	Photographed the Moon's surface for possible landing sites.
Luna 16 (USSR)	12 Sep 70	Made soft-landing, collected soil and returned it to USSR.
Luna 17 (USSR)	10 Nov 70	Landed Lunokhod 1, a roving vehicle for experiments controlled from Earth. It travelled for nearly a year.

Flying high

On April 12, 1961, the Russian astronaut Yuri Gagarin became the first person to travel in space. His spacecraft, called Vostok, circled Earth once, reaching a height of 203 miles, (327 km), and then landed on Earth again. The flight lasted about 89 minutes and proved that people could travel in space.

Off target

A mistake of only 1 mph (1.6 kph) in the Apollo's top speed would have led to it missing the Moon by about 1,000 miles (1,600 km). This is about the distance between Moscow and Berlin.

DID YOU KNOW?

The first living creature in space was a dog called Laika, launched in a spacecraft by the USSR in 1957. It died when its oxygen ran out.

A year in space

The world's most travelled person is the Soviet astronaut Valery Ryumin. His total time in space is 362 days, nearly a year. During his space trips he went around the world 5,750 times, covering 150 million miles (241 million km), more than the distance from Earth to Mars and back again.

Man on the Moon		
Spacecraft	Date	Results
Apollo 11 (USA)	16-24 July 69	Landed the first man on the Moon.
Apollo 12 (USA)	12-24 Nov 69	32 hour stay on the Moon.
Apollo 13 (USA)	11-17 Apr 70	Explosion in the spacecraft. Astronauts returned to Earth before landing.
Apollo 14 (USA)	31 Jan-9 Feb 71	Highland area of the Moon explored.
Apollo 15 (USA)	26 July-7 Aug 71	A car called a Lunar Rover taken to the Moon. Astronauts travelled 17.4 miles (28 km).
Apollo 16 (USA)	16-27 Apr 72	Another Lunar Rover taken on mission.
Apollo 17 (USA)	7-19 Dec 72	The last and longest stay on the Moon.

Amazing But True

On Earth, an astronaut in his spacesuit weighs about 300 lb (135 kg). But on the Moon he is six times lighter at only 50 lb (23 kg) because the Moon has much less gravity than the Earth.

Big booster

The total power developed by the USA Saturn V booster rocket, used for all the Apollo missions to the Moon, was almost 9,000,000 lb (4,082,000 kg) of thrust. This is equal to the power of 50 Boeing 747 jumbo jets.

Lunar rubbish

The Apollo astronauts left the remains of six lunar landers, three lunar rover vehicles and more than 55 tons of litter on the Moon. The total cost of the Apollo missions to the Moon is estimated at $25,000 million, making this some of the most expensive rubbish in history.

Visiting the planets

Automatic equipment

Since 1962, America and the USSR have been launching unmanned spacecraft to investigate the other planets in our Solar System. They carry cameras to take pictures and equipment to measure the magnetic fields and radiation of the planets. They also measure the temperature of the planets.

Probes to the planets

Spacecraft	Launch date	Mission
Mariner 2 (USA)	27 Aug 62	First successful fly-by of Venus.
Mariner 4 (USA)	28 Nov 64	First successful fly-by of Mars.
Venera 4 (USSR)	12 Jun 67	First entry into Venus atmosphere.
Mariner 9 (USA)	30 May 71	First successful Mars orbiter.
Pioneer 10 (USA)	3 Mar 72	First successful fly-by of Jupiter.
Venera 8 (USSR)	27 Mar 72	Returned first data from Venus surface.
Pioneer 11 (USA)	6 Apr 73	Jupiter probe. First fly-by of Saturn.
Mariner 10 (USA)	3 Nov 73	First TV pictures of Venus and Mercury.
Venera 9 (USSR)	8 Jun 75	First pictures from surface of Venus.
Viking 1 (USA)	20 Aug 75	First successful Mars landing.
Viking 2 (USA)	9 Sep 75	Returned data from Mars surface.
Voyager 2 (USA)	20 Aug 77	Fly-by of Jupiter, Saturn, Uranus, Neptune.
Voyager 1 (USA)	5 Sep 77	Fly-by probe of Jupiter and Saturn.
Pioneer-Venus 1 (USA)	20 May 78	Orbited Venus.
Pioneer-Venus 2 (USA)	8 Aug 78	Analyzed atmosphere and clouds of Venus.
Venera 13 (USSR)	30 Oct 81	First color pictures of Venus' surface. First soil analysis.
Venera 14 (USSR)	4 Nov 81	Repeated Venus soil analysis.
Venera 15 (USSR)	June 1983	Orbited and mapped Venus surface.
Venera 16 (USSR)	June 1983	Orbited and mapped Venus surface.

A clearer picture

Mariner 10 took about 4,300 close-up photographs of Mercury during its three visits from 1974. Before this, telescopes on Earth could hardly see the surface of Mercury.

Voyager 1 passed Saturn's moon Titan at a distance of only 2,500 miles (4,000 km) from the surface. It was more than 946 million miles (1,524 million km) from Earth. Such accuracy is like shooting an arrow at an apple 6 miles (9.6 km) away and the arrow passing within 1 in (2.54 cm) of the apple.

Goodbye

Pioneer 10 is expected to become the first man-made object to leave our Solar System. It crossed Neptune's path in 1983 and it will eventually disappear into the depths of space.

Metal message

Pioneer 10 and 11 carry metal plaques with messages for any aliens that might intercept the probes. Each plaque shows a map of the Solar System, the location of our Sun and sketches of human beings.

Look out

In 1968 a piece of Russian rocket broke a house window in Southend-on-Sea, England. In 1978 two French farmers were nearly hit by a 44 lb (20 kg) piece of a Russian rocket that landed in a field.

Six hour fly-by

The Voyager spacecraft travelled under Saturn's ring system at almost 43,000 mph (69,000 kph). At this speed, a rocket would take just six hours to travel from the Earth to the Moon. This is about the time it takes to travel from London to Bahrain by jet airplane today.

By 1993 there will be over 7,000 pieces of space debris orbiting the Earth, consisting of discarded rocket stages and fragments of rockets and satellites that have broken up.

Mapping it out

In less than two years from 1978, the Pioneer-Venus spacecraft mapped 93 per cent of Venus' surface. More was mapped of Venus in that time than had been mapped of Earth up to the year 1800.

Making music

Voyager 1 and 2 carry long-playing records containing electronically coded pictures of the Earth, spoken greetings, sound effects and a selection of music from around the world.

The future in space

A new space age

The human race is about to enter a new age of travelling and living in space. Shuttles will one day make journeys into space as common as ordinary airplane flights today. Space cities holding thousands of people will circle the Earth, metals will be mined and future wars may be fought in space.

Living on the Moon

By the beginning of the next century, the first bases on the Moon with people living in them should have been started. Because of the expense of transporting goods to the Moon, edible plants will have to be grown on it and as many things as possible, such as water, oxygen and rubbish, will have to be recycled.

Space cities

Plans have been suggested for building giant colonies in space, housing thousands of people. The land areas would be on the inside surfaces of giant cylinders or wheels which would spin around to provide gravity similar to the Earth's. Inside, people could walk around as freely as on Earth and grow their own food.

Terraforming Mars

Some scientists believe that the atmosphere of Mars could be warmed up so that people could live and work there. In a process called terraforming, plants would be grown around the ice caps to absorb sunlight, warm the surface and melt the ice.

Greening the galaxy

One day special trees might be developed so that they can grow on comets. Seeds from the trees could drift across space to take root on other comets, starting a wave of "greening" throughout the galaxy so that human beings could live on distant planets.

Amazing But True

In order to supply Venus with water, some scientists believe that icy comets could be diverted into the carbon dioxide clouds that surround the planet. There they would be melted to make rivers and lakes.

Space factories

Materials such as special metals and glass and also some medicines that are impossible to make on Earth can be made in space because of the lack of gravity. Eventually whole industries may be moved from Earth and housed in the space cities.

First space product

The first product ever to be made in space and sold on Earth were tiny balls made of a type of rubber called latex and used to measure microscopic objects. They were all exactly the same size, but latex balls made on Earth can vary in size.

Energy from space

Some scientists believe that the Earth's electricity in the future could come from space. Giant groups of solar cells, which convert sunlight into electricity, would be placed about 22,300 miles (35,880 km) above the equator. The electricity generated by the solar cells would then be beamed down to Earth.

Mining in space

The world is beginning to run short of some essential metals and minerals such as iron and aluminium, but there are plentiful supplies of them elsewhere in the Solar System. One day our Moon and planets such as Mars and the asteroids will be mined for metals.

DID YOU KNOW?

Solar power stations would weigh at least 55,000 tons each, more than 600 times the weight of Skylab, the heaviest object ever launched into space. To build a power station in orbit around Earth would require about 5,000 flights of the Space Shuttle to carry the building materials.

Starships

The closest star to our Solar System is over four light years away. The journey in a rocket today would take nearly 200,000 years. Future rocket engines have been suggested that would use beams of light for power. These rockets could nearly reach the speed of light, so the same journey would take just over four years.

41

Is there life out there?

We are not alone

Some scientists believe that there are other civilizations in the Milky Way as well as ours. With about 100,000 million stars in our galaxy, it has been estimated that there may be up to one million planets on which there is life of some kind, such as animals or plants.

Am I receiving you?

In 1960, an American astronomer called Frank Drake made the first attempt to pick up possible messages from other stars. He turned a radio telescope to two stars, called Tau Ceti and Epsilon Eridani. Although he listened for two months, Drake received no messages from the stars.

Strange sights

For centuries there have been reports of strange lights in the sky, craft landing on Earth and creatures emerging from them. Recently, sightings of UFOs (unidentified flying objects) have increased. Most are easily explained, but some remain mysteries.

Are you receiving me?

Since 1974, a radio message beamed from the Arecibo radio telescope in Puerto Rico has been racing toward a cluster of 300,000 stars known as M13. The stars are so far away that even if there are any creatures living in M13, their answer will not reach Earth until about the year 50,000.

The pattern of the Arecibo message

Some famous UFOs

1254. A mysterious colored ship is supposed to have appeared over St. Albans, England.

1741. Lord Beauchamp saw a small oval ball of fire descending from the sky in England. It then vanished.

1762. A thin UFO surrounded by a glowing ring was spotted by two astronomers near Basle, Switzerland.

1820. A stream of saucer-shaped objects crossed the town of Embrun, France.

1947. A pilot reported seeing gleaming discs flying over the Rocky Mountains. He described them as "skipping like saucers across water" and the name "flying saucer" caught on.

1971. Two men in the USA claimed to have been captured and taken on board a flying saucer where they were examined by tall creatures.

Amazing But True

Over the last 30 years over 100,000 people have reported UFO experiences. A public opinion poll carried out in the USA in 1974 showed that more than one in ten people questioned claimed to have seen a UFO.

A vintage year

1952 was a very good year for UFO sightings. There were about 1,500 reports of UFOs from different parts of the world. Most of these sightings have simple explanations, such as airplanes, clouds or bright stars, but many remain unexplained.

Swedish sightings

In 1946 in Sweden alone there were about 1,000 reports of UFOs. Most of the reports were of rocket-shaped objects, which have never been identified.

Lines in the sand

At Nazca in Peru there is a plain covered by very straight and wide tracks in the rocky surface up to 5 miles (8 km) long. Seen from above, they look like an airfield. They may be connected with early astronomy, but it is unlikely that they were used as runways by UFOs, as some people claim.

Putting up statues

Some people believe that the giant statues on Easter Island in the Pacific Ocean were put up with the help of visitors from space. But scientists believe that it would have been possible for the islanders to have erected them without any outside help.

DID YOU KNOW?

UFOs are usually seen between 9 pm and 10:30 pm. They have been reported from every country in the world. News of them flows in at an average of 40 sightings every day.

UFO spotting in space

The first UFO seen in space was spotted by the astronaut James McDivitt through the window of the Gemini 4 spacecraft in 1965. He saw an object with arms sticking out of it about 9.5 miles (15 km) from the capsule.

Astronomy lists

Famous observatories

Name	Country	Type
Arecibo	Puerto Rico	Radio
Byurakan	Armenia	Optical
Cambridge	England	Radio
Cerro Tololo	Chile	Optical
Flagstaff	USA	Optical
Green Bank	USA	Radio
La Palma	Canary Islands	Optical
Jodrell Bank	England	Radio
Kitt Peak	USA	Optical
Mauna Kea	Hawaii	Optical
Mt Palomar	USA	Optical
Parkes	Australia	Radio
Pulkovo	Russia	Optical
Siding Spring	Australia	Optical
Zelenchukskaya	Russia	Optical

Meteor showers

Name	Date
Quadrantids	Jan 1-5
April Lyrids	Apr 19-24
Aquarids	May 1-8
June Lyrids	June 10-21
Perseids	July 25-Aug 18
Cygnids	Aug 18-22
Orionids	Oct 16-27
Taurids	Oct 10-Dec 5
Leonids	Nov 14-20
Geminids	Dec 7-15

The largest asteroids

Name	Diameter (km)	(miles)
Ceres	1,000	620
Pallas	610	380
Vesta	540	340
Hygeia	450	280
Euphrosyne	370	230
Interamnia	350	220
Davida	330	200
Cybele	310	190
Europa	290	180
Patientia	280	170
Eunomia	270	165
Psyche	250	155

Future solar total eclipses

Date	Approximate location	Approximate duration
3 Nov 1994	Central South America, South Atlantic	4 minutes
24 Oct 1995	South Asia, Central Pacific	2 minutes
9 March 1997	Central Asia	3 minutes
26 Feb 1998	Central Pacific, northern South America	4 minutes
11 Aug 1999	North Atlantic, Central Europe, South Asia	2 minutes
21 June 2001	Atlantic, South Africa	5 minutes
4 Dec 2002	South Africa, Indian Ocean, Australia	2 minutes
23 Nov 2003	Antarctica	2 minutes
8 Apr 2005	Pacific, America, northern South America	1 minute

Our local group of galaxies

Leo I	NGC6822
Leo II	NGC185
Large Magellanic Cloud	IC1613
	Wolf-Lundmark
Sculptor	Triangulum
Fornax	NGC147
Milky Way	M32
Small Magellanic Cloud	Andromeda
	NGC205

Major astronomical satellites

OSO 4
18 Oct, 1967
Orbiting Solar
Observatory

OAO 2
7 Dec, 1968
Orbiting
Astronomical
Observatory, for
ultraviolet
observations

SAS 1
12 Dec, 1970
Small Astronomy
Satellite, made x-ray
survey of sky

TD-1A
12 March, 1972
European high
energy
astronomy satellite

OAO 3
21 Aug, 1972
Orbiting
Astronomical
Observatory, for
ultraviolet and x-ray
studies

SAS 2
15 Nov, 1972
Small Astronomy
Satellite, made
gamma-ray survey

Ariel V
15 Oct, 1974
UK x-ray satellite

SAS 3
7 May, 1975
Small Astronomy
Satellite, studied
x-ray sources

OSO 8
21 June, 1975
Orbiting Solar
Observatory

HEAO 1
12 Aug, 1977
High Energy
Astronomy
Observatory, made
x-ray survey

IUE
26 Jan, 1978
International
Ultraviolet Explorer,
joint ESA/NASA
satellite

HEAO 2
13 Nov, 1978
High Energy
Astronomy
Observatory
examined
individual x-ray
sources

Ariel VI
2 June, 1979
UK satellite for
cosmic ray and x-ray
studies

HEAO 3
20 Sept, 1979
High Energy
Astronomy
Observatory for
gamma-ray studies

SMM
14 Feb, 1980
Solar Maximum
Mission,
to study the Sun

IRAS
25 Jan, 1983
Infra-red satellite
to provide complete
survey of the sky

Hipparcos
8 Aug 1989
Accurate
measurements of
positions of stars

COBE
18 Nov 1989
Cosmic Background
Explorer
Studies of radiation
left from Big Bang

ROSAT
1 June 1990
Roentgen Satellite
all sky x-ray and
ultraviolet survey

Hubble Space
Telescope
25 Aug 1990
Orbiting
astronomical
telescope

Gamma Ray
Observatory
6 Apr 1991
survey at all gamma-
ray wavelengths

EUVE
7 June 1992
Extreme Ultra Violet
explorer
mapping sky in
extreme ultraviolet
radiation

Space words

Astronomical unit The average distance from Earth to the Sun, about 93 million miles (150 million km).

Constellation A group of stars which appear to make a shape or pattern in the sky. The stars were joined up to make the outlines of mythical animals or people. There are 88 constellations.

Eclipse This occurs when the Earth passes between the Sun and the Moon and light from the Sun is cut off (a lunar eclipse). It also happens when the Moon passes between the Sun and the Earth, casting a shadow on the Earth (a solar eclipse).

Galaxy A giant group of stars held together by gravity. The largest galaxies contain up to a million, million stars.

Gravity All objects in space attract each other by gravity. It is the invisible pull of the Earth which keeps the Moon in orbit around it, and the pull of the Sun which keeps the Earth and the other planets in their orbits around the Sun.

Light year The distance light travels in one year, 5.9 million, million miles (9,460,000 million km).

Nebula A cloud of gas and dust, sometimes dotted with clusters and stars. Stars may be born in nebulae.

Orbit The curved path taken by a natural or man-made object as it moves around another object.

Planet An object which has no light of its own but shines by reflecting a star's light.

Pulsar Very small, fast-spinning star which sends out a flash of radio waves as it spins around.

Quasar An extremely bright and distant object, much smaller than a galaxy but thousands of times brighter.

Radio telescope A special kind of telescope designed to collect radio waves from space.

Red shift The reddening of the light from a star, indicating it is moving away.

Satellite A natural or artificial object that circles around another. The Moon is a natural satellite of the Earth.

Solar System The system of our Sun. It consists of the nine planets and their moons, the asteroids and comets, all of which orbit the Sun.

Solar wind The high-speed stream of electrically-charged atoms of gas sent out by the Sun.

Star A ball of gas that produces its own heat and light from nuclear reactions at its center

Universe Everything which is known or thought to exist in space.

Index

ISBN 0-590-22512-X

First published in Great Britain in 1987 by Usborne Publishing Ltd. Copyright © 1987 by Usborne Publishing Ltd. All rights reserved. Published by Scholastic Inc., 555 Broadway, New York, NY 10012, by arrangement with Usborne Publishing Ltd.

12 11 10   1 2 3 4 5 6/0

Printed in the U.S.A.
First Scholastic printing, February 1995

23